JEWISH AS A SECOND LANGUAGE

JEWISH AS A SECOND LANGUAGE

By Molly Katz

Illustrated by
Jeff Moores

WORKMAN PUBLISHING, NEW YORK

For Bill, my inspiration.

ACKNOWLEDGMENTS

I'm grateful to Sally Kovalchick, my superb editor, as well as to Peter Workman and my wonderful agent, Henry Morrison . . . thank you all for your efforts and your support, and for loving a good laugh.

Thanks as well to the friends and relatives, current and former, who contributed to this book, wittingly and otherwise.

Copyright © 1991 by Molly Katz
Illustrations copyright © 1991 by Jeff Moores

Library of Congress Cataloging-in-Publication Data

Katz, Molly.
Jewish as a second language / by Molly Katz
p.   cm.
ISBN 0-89480-885-0
1. Jewish wit and humor.   2. American wit and humor.   3. Jews-United States —
Social life and customs — Humor.   I. Title
PN6231.J5K38 1991   90-21510
                                                CIP

Book design by Stefanie Rosenfeld

Workman Publishing
708 Broadway
New York, New York 10003
Manufactured in the United States
of America
First printing March 1991
10 9 8 7 6 5 4 3 2 1

CONTENTS

▼

INTRODUCTION

Part 1
DEVELOPING JEWISH CONVERSATIONAL SKILLS

Part 2
THE JEWISH HOME

Part 3

ENTERTAINMENT

Part 4
YOUR NEW JEWISH BODY

Part 5
BUILDING YOUR NEW JEWISH ECONOMIC PERSPECTIVE

PART 6
RAISING YOUR JEWISH CHILD

Part 7
JOINING IN THE CUSTOMS OF YOUR NEW JEWISH FAMILY

Part 8
READINESS TEST

INTRODUCTION

▼

I am Jewish. My husband Bill is Not. One day my mother had to get her blood pressure checked. She didn't need a ride, she said; she'd call a cab. Bill said, "Okay."

Of course, she stopped speaking to us.

"How could you?" I asked Bill.

"How could I what?"

"Let her take a cab."

"But," Bill said, "it was her idea."

"You should have known how to translate," I said.

He said, "*My* mother would have taken a cab."

"She's not Jewish. If a Jewish person offers to take a cab, she never *means* it."

"Well, you'll have to be patient with me," he said. "Jewish is only my second language."

Not your religion. ("She's Jewish, but her husband's Not.")

ONCE, nobody married Jews except other Jews (and rich, neurotic non-Jews trying to torture their Patrician families after all other methods, such as working in a live-sex show, had failed).

But there are many of you out there now, non-Jews swimming in the rubber cement of our mores, and you need help. There is much to learn about things you thought you already knew how to do, such as talk, think, eat, feel and behave. Keeping a low profile, in the hope that your new lifestyle will evolve smoothly if you're observant and tactful, is about as effective as walking into a panther cage with a shoelace for a whip.

To learn the Jewish language, you need to understand one point especially: this does not mean Yiddish, the Eastern European language derived from German with which we Jews often pepper our English. You'll never have to speak Yiddish, except to stumble over a word or phrase occasionally with the awkwardness expected of you.

Jews know you're uncomfortable with Yiddish. We know you feel left out. As well you should: it's designed to *keep* you out.

We like to believe your tongue can't form the tangles of consonants necessary to say a Yiddish word. Therefore, no matter how it comes out, you'll be corrected. One of us will explain to you that *gonif*, the way you pronounced it, doesn't simply mean thief, but a Bosnian thief who steals your sister's ankle bracelet.

Don't try to improve your pronunciation, though. Instead, learn just enough about Yiddish to make your errors truly hysterical. This effort will pay off in family relations: your in-laws will have a blast hooting at your mistakes (which they know you'll find endearing).

Be sure your usage is faulty, too. This confirms our conviction that Yiddish defies translation, that mere English can't match its intricate layers of meaning — and

On Joining a Jewish Family

Disadvantages	Advantages
You'll never have a brother-in-law who can replace your voltage regulator.	You won't have to look at tattoos.
You'll need to keep a straight face when someone orders a Virgin Colada.	Your spouse won't die of cirrhosis.
You'll have to sell your bowling ball.	You'll never have to climb a ladder.
You'll never travel to anyplace that isn't hot.	You'll always have an accountant.
You can kiss caffeine goodbye.	You'll eat the best baked goods money can buy.
You'll have to scrape off all your hilarious bumper stickers.	No one will give your child an ant farm.
No one in the family will get drunk with you when the Yankees win the pennant.	There will always be plenty of sweaters in the house. Any house.
No one in the family will get drunk with you when the Yankees lose the pennant.	You'll never have to live with indoor-outdoor carpeting, aluminum siding, or an aboveground pool.
No one in the family will get drunk with you.	Your in-laws will insist on believing your forebears settled Plymouth Rock, even if the only ancestor you know of was a hashish-addicted pederast from Flanders.

HIC!

YANKEES LOSE

that non-Jews are hopeless when they try to use it. We love to hear you deliver howlers like "When she found out she wasn't invited, she made such a big *schmatta* you could hear her down the street" or "Put everything on my bagel—nova, onions, the whole *schlemiel.*"*

No, the true language of Jews is not Yiddish. It is the complex twists and somersaults of everyday American conversation, the swamps and thickets of behavior. It is nuances and expectations, hidden meanings and unvoiced point systems . . . wins, losses and draws in competitions you had no idea you'd entered.

This book is your guide to the mysterious web of your new environment. Study it carefully, and the secrets of our language will unfold.

---

*What the Yiddish really means:

Schmatta: a rag ("Oh, this? Just a *schmatta* I picked up at Dior").
Schlemiel: a poor fool ("What a *schlemiel!* He thinks she bought that *schmatta* wholesale").

Part 1

DEVELOPING JEWISH CONVERSATIONAL SKILLS

HOW TO IDENTIFY A GOOD CONVERSATION

▼

Forget the clichés you've heard about Jews' love of learning. What we love more than that is *talking*, so plan on doing a monumental amount of it. You'll be holding conversations with your in-laws, with friends of the family, with everyone *they* converse with. Here's how to make sure you know what you're doing.

▶ By now you've had twenty-odd years in which to finish your sentences. This is enough for anybody. We hope you enjoyed the luxury while you had it, because you'll never finish one again. Nor would you want to. The more interruptions, the more enthusiastic the conversation. Three or four people talking at once is ideal. This is your signal of acceptance. If no one jumps in to join the fun, it means that what you're saying is boring.

▶ Another indication that your new family enjoys conversing with you is when they ask lots of friendly questions. Things like "How come your parents were divorced?" and "Is it true your uncle went bankrupt?" are signs that they're really taking an interest.

▶ You'll know you're a truly valued conversational partner when they do you the honor of sharing crucial points of advice. Observations such as "You look nauseating in peach" or "That haircut emphasizes your double chin" should erase any insecurity you may still have about your role as a companion in repartee.

WHERE TO CONVERSE

▼

Whether we're talking with friends, acquaintances, clerks or total strangers, the most enjoyable Jewish conversations are impromptu. They occur in the following locations.

At the Supermarket. When you run into a friend here, of course you must catch up. Select a narrow aisle piled with cartons. Position your shopping baskets so no one can get by. Feel free to chat as long and as loudly as you wish. Ignore the glares of other shoppers — they're just jealous of the good time you're having.

In a Department Store. The salesclerk showing you a lipstick will be glad to wait while you catch up with the friend who's just greeted you. That's what she's there for. Never be so rude as to exclude her from your talk. If your friend doesn't think to get the clerk's input on her upcoming hysterectomy, *you* do it.

In a Restaurant. If you see people you know, hurry to the table no matter what stage of their meal it is. They'll be eager to chat with you and introduce their tablemates. Make sure everyone joins the conversation. They can eat anytime.

At a Party. Ignore all the guests you don't know; they can talk to their *own* friends. Scream to familiar faces to come join you. Spend the entire evening trying to outyell one another on the most inconsequential topics. You'll know you're doing this correctly when the room rings with shouts like "What do you *mean* you haven't fertilized your lawn all summer?"

On a Waiting Line. Jews love lines. Aside from the fact that finding one at the movie or other event we've picked confirms the brilliance of our choice, we consider a waiting line our personal studio audience.

As soon as you reach the line, ask the person in front of you if he or she is the end. Ask as many other questions as you can think of, even if the person obviously knows no more than you do. When you're out of questions, begin talking to whoever you came with. Keep up a running dialogue about everyone walking by and everything happening around you. Do this in a tone so loud that others on line know they're expected to join the conversation. With practice, you can hone this technique so exquisitely that bystanders feel guilty for keeping silent.

11 WAYS *NOT* TO START A CONVERSATION WITH A JEWISH PERSON

▼

1. "How do you get rid of pinworms?"
2. "I put miniature marshmallows in my coleslaw."
3. "Is that real, or zirconia?"
4. "A priest, a minister and a rabbi were in a lifeboat . . ."
5. "Where can I get a deal on a Harley?"
6. "Got a bus schedule on you?"
7. "I forgot to put this tuna salad in the refrigerator. It's still good, isn't it?"
8. "What's your favorite campground?"
9. "No more bounced checks for me. Household Finance came through."
10. "There's nothing like a Timex."
11. "Them Bruins gonna win the Stanley Cup?"

CONVERSATIONAL STRATEGY

▼

An essential element of your new communication skills is the ability to make statements that express the opposite of what you mean. This is generally done in two ways.

1. The Positive Insult. A comment that masquerades as a putdown but, properly translated, makes the other person feel good.

Apparent Insult	Translation
"This Queen Anne table is so pretentious."	"I wish I could afford it."
"Isn't your Jessica wearing too much blush?"	"Too bad my Hilary has a face like a waffle iron."
"That brocade suit is much too dressy for a brunch."	"I wish I could afford it."
"How can you eat this junk? It's full of cholesterol."	"If I weren't twenty-five pounds overweight, I'd eat it, too."
"You're crazy to buy a Jag. They break down in the rain."	"I wish I could afford it."

nice an all-purpose, meaningless adjective. ("I'm dying of thirst. Bring me a nice glass of water.")

2. The Negative Compliment. The reverse of the positive insult; a candy-coated torpedo.

Apparent Compliment	Translation
"How wonderful that you and Milton can get away so often."	"Some of us work for a living."
"What a fudge cake! You must have put in a pound of butter."	"I'm going to be up all night with diarrhea."
"Your husband is such a fabulous dancer."	"How come he married a klutz?"
"I love how your diamond reflects the light."	"Just *say* you're engaged to a cardiologist. You don't have to blind us."

TELEPHONE CONVERSATION

▼

Few accessories are as vital to Jewish life as the telephone. This auditory pacemaker has its own set of etiquette rules.

1. When making a call, converse with someone near you as you dial. Be in the middle of a sentence as your party answers. Complete the sentence before greeting your party.

Repeat the procedure when answering the phone. When this is done properly, the caller will hear a greeting such as "—hate playing tennis when I have my period. Hello?"

2. Remember, it's rude to talk on the phone with nothing in your mouth. Always have something crunchy like a toasted English muffin on hand in case the phone rings. Take large bites and chew audibly, pausing only when the other person is speaking.

THE QUINTESSENTIAL JEWISH PHONE CONVERSATION

"Hi. I'm returning your call to tell you I can't call you."

"That's okay. I only took the call to tell you I can't take your call."

3. Have frequent side conversations. Scream at some-one several rooms away without moving your mouth from the receiver.

4. Put your caller on hold as often as possible. Do you want people to think no one else calls you?

Jewish Phraseology

A verage, humdrum things never happen to Jews. Even the weather isn't the same for us as it is for others, regardless of the fact that it's the same wea-ther. Accordingly, all our expressions are maximums, superlatives and extremes.

You used to:	But now you:
Get caught in the rain	Get drenched in a downpour
Have a headache	Have a terrible headache
Be tired	Are totally exhausted
Taste something good	Have discovered something absolutely fabulous
Be warm or cold	Are boiling or freezing
Say a road was slippery	Say it's a sheet of ice
Be hungry	Are starving to death
Be surprised	Have cardiac arrest
Feel anxious	Are shaking like a leaf
Be allergic	Are violently allergic

BODY LANGUAGE

▼

Y ou undoubtedly watch in awe as your new relatives converse among themselves, using not just their voices but as many body parts as are humanly movable. To join in, you'll need to master these communication skills.

The Shrugs

A shrug is achieved by lifting the shoulders. It may be accompanied by your choice of faces and hand movements (see below). The intensity of the shrugged emotion is indicated by the degree to which the neck is hidden. When practicing shrugs, be sure to wear a little sweater to ward off muscle spasms.

The Basic Four Shrugs

▶ Incredulous ("I was supposed to know it would rain?")

▶ Helpless ("Me? Lift *that*?")

▶ Stymied ("Look it up in the dictionary.")

▶ All-purpose ("Go know.")

The Faces

▶ Pained ("That's the best you can do?")

▶ Bug-eyed ("*How* much?")

▶ Aggrieved ("No letter, no call, nothing.")

▶ Dissatisfied ("I said paint it *light* persimmon, not dark.")

▶ Shocked ("Rejected? *Me?*")

▶ Pleased ("I told you that chair would break if you stood on it.")

The Hands

▶ Waving ("Doctor, schmoctor. He's an *optometrist.*")

▶ Raised, palms out ("Stop *yelling.*")

▶ Extended ("Would I lie?")

▶ On head ("*Now* what?")

▶ Applauding ("You finally got it right.")

UNDERSTANDING JEWISH CHITCHAT

▼

To fully appreciate conversing with your new family, you will need to learn our unique Jewish expressions and familiarize yourself with some eccentric usage.

Basic Vocabulary

crime a little bit of a shame. ("It's a crime to waste these nectarines.")

little sweater a cardigan. For no known reason, it is never called just a sweater. It has curative and protective powers. ("I'm freezing in here. Get me a little sweater." Or, "Take a little sweater so you don't catch a chill.").

ifGodforbid an advance antidote. Since God monitors everything Jews say, it's vital not to give Him any ideas. You must signal Him so He'll know what you *don't* want ("ifGodforbid Sol should lose one of his stores . . .")

THE BAKERY RAN OUT OF ONION RYE. IT'S A CRIME.

nausea a state of being that has nothing to do with the stomach. ("I tried Neiman's. Their gowns were nauseating." Or, "We had to let the Lincoln go for sixteen-two. We were nauseous.")

Oddities of Usage

You must tune your ear to some new verbal twists. The present tense, for example, is used to express the passage of time. The answer to "How long are you married?" is not "Until death do us part" but "Three years." The answer to "How long do you have this roof leak?" is "Since I'm living here."

Other peculiarities include:

1. The contraction, preceded by "so" and accompanied by a shrug, used to express the obvious solution to a problem:

▶ "What if Melissa doesn't get into Harvard?"
"So she'll go to Yale."

▶ "My car is in the shop."
"So you'll rent one."

2. The verb, a part of speech with which their sentences Jews often end:

▶ "If he runs out of money, so he'll call and you'll send."

▶ "There's cheesecake left. Who doesn't have?"
"I don't have."
"So come over here and get."

3. What ——, used with the emphasis on the second word to underscore the ludicrousness of a notion:

▶ "We'll give Jason AT&T stock for graduation."
"What *stock*? We'll give him a Camaro."

▶ "I heard your sister bought a beach cottage."
"What *cottage*? It's a tri-level contemporary with six and a half baths."

The One Phrase You'll Never Hear a Jewish Person Utter

"NO PROBLEM"

Because:
1. There is no such thing as a situation that is not a problem, and
2. No Jewish person would suggest a favor isn't being done when one is.

Part 2
THE JEWISH HOME

DECORATION

▼

Now that you have a Jewish home, you must make sure it looks like one, i.e., like everyone else's in the family. Jews get insecure in unfamiliar settings. To ensure your relative's comfort, and establish the appropriate surrounding for your new lifestyle, make certain your home conforms, visually and functionally, in these essential ways.

Broadloom. A generic word for floor covering, the purpose of which is to keep you worrying about preventing dents in the pile. Furniture legs never rest on it, but on plastic circles. So that the circles won't make dents, they sit on nice little squares of broadloom atop the actual broadloom. While broadloom may be used in most any room, it is always found in the . . .

Living Room. A display of fragile furniture, paintings and a grand piano. No one ever plays the piano. The paintings often have viewing lights, which are never turned on. Since the room isn't entered except to be cleaned, no living is done here. It is done in the . . .

Family Room. An area whose focus derives from that favorite Jewish activity, *sitting*. All furniture is chosen and upholstered in terms of how good it is for *sitting*. The floor covering must be comfortable to *sit* on. The TV and stereo are positioned according to where those using them will *sit*. The family room is a vital part of your house, but definitely secondary to the . . .

Bathroom. The heart of the Jewish home. It is here that one is cleaned, inside and out, and this room must be decorated and supplied in line with the importance of what takes place within its walls. Spare no expense acquir-

ing the thickest towels, the softest toilet paper.

A new family member who is truly committed to Jewish life must become completely self-absorbed in the performance of bathroom functions. You'll know you've mastered this when you find yourself discussing toilet habits and gastrointestinal events as avidly as if they were election bulletins.

COLORS

There are two categories of Jewish colors.

1. Edible Nouns. A couch of *mushroom* watered silk matches drapes with a thread of *salmon*. A *currant* bath rug complements *eggplant* towels.

2. Meaningless Nouns. These give you no idea what the color is: *taupe, ecru, slate, teal, umber, mist.*

Some colors are never Jewish, such as aqua.

Decorating Guidelines

▶ Never use a decorator. If you do, say you didn't.

▶ Choose completely impractical pale colors and gossamer fabrics for your living room. This enables you to hover and fret whenever someone is in danger of sitting on the furniture or walking on the broadloom.

▶ Order floor-to-ceiling draperies for the living room and bedrooms. Do this even if the windows are small. Do it even if there aren't any windows.

▶ Buy stiff designer bedding, inflexible decorative pillows, and the costliest top-name granite-firm mattresses. All your beds will now be impossible to sleep on, but no matter. They're the best.

▶ You would never be so crass as to select artwork by any artificial criterion. But can you help it if the paintings you fall in love with just happen to match your color scheme?

▶ Furnish your formal dining room with a table big enough to host an inauguration banquet. Never, Godforbid, use it. It is an ironclad Jewish tradition to squeeze guests around a kitchen table while the dining room set gleams in empty splendor.

YOUR JEWISH KITCHEN

▼

Your primary kitchen responsibility is to keep the room looking as if it's never used. Since a Jewish kitchen is used a great deal, this is difficult, but with practice you'll learn the proper rhythm.

▶ Have a sponge in your hand at all times. Immediately wipe up any drop of anything that spills anywhere.

▶ It is not enough to simply wash dishes. Scrub them clean before putting them in the dishwasher.

▶ Don't leave a dirty dish for a microsecond. From the moment you remove it clean from its cabinet, your goal is to use, wash, dry and return it as swiftly as is humanly possible.

▶ Think of a creative place to hide your trash can. You'll know you have a good spot when someone trying to find it has to open six doors and finally ask where it is.

▶ Constantly mop the floor. People *walk* there, for God's sake.

Kitchen Terms You Need to Know

not sanitary acceptable for a research laboratory or operating room, but not for a Jewish kitchen. ("Don't eat that grape you dropped on the counter. It's not sanitary.")

on the stove in imminent danger of being ruined by overcooking. ("Come home right now! Dinner's on the stove!")

on the table about to spoil. ("Hurry up and sit down! Dinner's on the table!")

cold worse than spoiled. ("Eat! Eat! It's going to get *cold*!")

Kitchen Equipment

Small Appliances. Have them for every purpose — an electric knife, food processor, can opener, meat slicer, coffee grinder, blender, etc. But don't use any of them. Explain with a weary smile that the job is easier/faster/tastier/more sanitary if done by hand.

Perfect Containers for Leftovers (pickle-size for pickles, elongated for celery, etc.). These are sturdy something-thingware bowls and boxes shaped for every conceivable food. They have lock-on lids and vacuum seals. They're guaranteed to maintain freshness for weeks, but no Jewish person would believe such bushwa. Empty yours after twelve hours.

A beautiful, gleaming, costly, high-tech electric coffeemaker that makes absolutely putrid coffee.

Cookbooks. Have several shelves of these. Keep adding the most current ones. Lug them from house to house as you move. Never open them.

A Spice Rack. A decorative shelf containing pretty bottles. Mount yours on a wall or on a countertop. Do not, Godforbid, use any of the spices in it. Do you want to be doubled over with gas pains?

A Spoon Rest. This is a concave plastic flower kept on the counter. The spoon used to stir a cooking pot is rested there between stirrings. If you have difficulty understanding why having yet another sticky, dirty item to wash after a big meal is preferable to simply wiping the counter, this is because you weren't born Jewish.

17 ITEMS YOU WON'T SEE IN A JEWISH HOME

▼

1. A TV tray
2. Bowling shoes
3. A one-size-fits-all garment
4. A painting of kittens with big eyes
5. A linoleum knife
6. Chef Boy-Ar-Dee
7. A standby ticket
8. Trout flies
9. A peek-a-boo nightie
10. Boxing gloves
11. A copy of *Smart Women, Foolish Choices*
12. Krazy Mixed-Up Salt
13. A snow shovel
14. Count Chocula
15. The *Time-Life War Library*
16. A poo-poo cushion
17. A Rottweiler

VISITING SOMEONE'S HOME

▼

I n your pre-Jewish years, people invited you to their homes for many purposes — tennis, swimming, cards, garden projects. Your new family will want to have you over, too, but only for one activity: eating.

Don't assume that because you've had plenty of experience with both visiting and eating, this will be a simple area to master. Be on the alert for the following surprises.

Bet-You-Never-Thought-I-Could-Make-You-Feel-This-Guilty

You: "Sorry we're late. We hit traffic."

Your hostess: "My God, I never should have told you to come at four!"

Y: "It's okay. We just — "

YH: "What a total idiot I am! I forgot about the pool traffic! God! I can't do anything right!"

Y: "Nonsense. Everything's fine."

YH: "Watch the chicken. I'm going to take a Valium."

The Perishables Rodeo

As a guest in a Jewish home, you are obligated to notice and call attention to perishable foods left out of the refrigerator.

To do this, you must learn to identify the odor of a dish that might be starting to come close to nearing the condition of possibly approaching the likelihood of beginning to spoil within the next few weeks.

After you've been in your new Jewish family awhile, you'll automatically respond with horror anytime the word *perishable* is uttered. Its nearest synonym is *botulism*. When a Jewish person notes that a food is perishable, it is assumed to have already perished.

Jewish Guest Behavior

When visiting your new relatives and friends, you will encounter situations that seem familiar. Your impulse will be to handle them in the familiar way. Don't make this mistake.

Here are some lessons.

SITUATION 1 (WOMEN ONLY)

You've brought your special coconut pie to the dinner party. As you arrive, your hostess is dashing around the kitchen preparing the meal.

Old Behavior. You discreetly slip the pie into the refrigerator and leave the kitchen.

New Behavior. Loudly announce you've brought the pie as soon as you walk in. Keep talking on your way to the kitchen. Grab the hostess and show her. Tell her how you made it. Don't leave out any of the delicious details. Ask where the cream is. Have her get a beater so you can whip the cream. Show her how you grate the coconut on top. When you're done, take things out of the refrigerator to make room for the pie. Leave them out.

SITUATION 2 (WOMEN ONLY)

You're at a new relative's holiday dinner. Nearly everyone has finished eating. You'd like to help clear.

Old Behavior. You wait till the last person is done, then carry plates to the kitchen. Everyone moves to the living room. Later, before leaving, you offer to help wash. The hostess declines.

New Behavior. About now the hostess will rise and reach for the plates of those who are finished. Stand next to her and help as she scrapes food onto one plate and stacks the others. Keep glancing at those still eating to see if they're done yet. Only when all

How to Comment on Someone's Home

About outdoor furniture: *"You're going to cover this?"*

About dark carpeting: *"But it shows the dirt."*

About a new appliance (with a knowing sigh): *"Save the warranty."*

About an exquisitely decorated nursery (with eyes rolled): *"Wait."*

About a white anything: *"You're going to cover this?"*

dishes are scraped, stacked and organized can you bring them to the kitchen.

The men, and any women who don't care about their reputations, will retire to the family room for TV and conversation about what's on the TV. The real women will bulldoze the kitchen, washing, wiping and wrapping leftover food to the tune of such favorites as "It's a Crime to Throw This Out," "Let the Glasses Air-Dry—It's More Sanitary" and "Don't You Have a Tupperware Scallion Container?"

SITUATION 3

You're a dinner guest. You've brought a huge tin of anchovies for a gift (you have a relative in the restaurant-supply business).

Old Behavior. You present the gift, eat and leave.

New Behavior. Before the dinner, mention often that you're bringing something great. When you arrive, insist that the hostess serve the anchovies immediately. Ask if she has capers. Suggest she roll each anchovy around one. Watch while she does it. She might miss some.

Direct the other guests' attention to the anchovies. Don't let them get distracted by the other hors d'oeuvres. During the meal, remind everyone a few times how good the anchovies were. When you leave, ask the hostess if she *really* enjoyed them. Hint that you might bring something even better next time.

SITUATION 4

You're a guest at Roz's dinner party. As she serves the first course, Roz announces: "This is terrible soup."

Old Behavior. N/A. Situation is exclusive to Jewish gatherings.

New Behavior. Say nothing. Roz always does this, and the other guests all know their lines. You'll hear "Why does she always do this?", "We haven't even tasted it" and "You're right, Roz, we already hate the whole meal." Anything you said would be as disruptive as if you leaped onstage during *La Bohème* and sang "Shimmy Shimmy Ko Ko Bop."

SITUATION 5

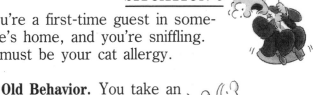

You're a first-time guest in someone's home, and you're sniffling. It must be your cat allergy.

Old Behavior. You take an antihistamine and have fun anyway.

New Behavior. Ask accusingly if they have a cat. Announce that you're violently allergic. When they offer to put the cat in another room, say it's too late. Ask what medications they have. Reject them all. Describe the details of your allergy. Use up a box or two of tissues. When the topic shifts, sneeze louder.

Things You Can Count on Hearing Around the Table

▶ "But that's the best part!" (Said while pointing at a broccoli stem or scaly, footlike hunk of chicken left on your plate.)

▶ "Sit down, [hostess]! She never sits down!" (Always said by someone who never gets up.)

▶ "I should have made more."

▶ "You always make too much."

▶ "Don't fill up on the bread." (Said by parents to children, spouses to each other, and the hostess to everybody.)

Part 3
ENTERTAINMENT

WORRYING

▼

Before you were Jewish, you probably spent time each day on your entertainment — jogging, painting, reading. You are fortunate to have this routine established, because it won't be hard to fit in your new entertainment — worrying. Of course, you'll have to forgo the jogging, but which is more important?

Natural-born Jews leave the womb equipped with a worry reservoir that is filled early and replenished constantly. We worry about everything. Worrying is as essential to our well-being as a balanced breakfast. It is our duty, our birthright, and our most profound satisfaction. There are no exceptions to this rule. *All Jews worry all the time.* If there is nothing handy to worry about, we are breath-stoppingly creative at finding something.

You will need daily practice to build your worrying skills. Think of this as weight training.

How to Worry

You may choose from three basic methodologies.

Personal. Select an inconsequential remark someone makes to you. Magnify it out of all proportion. Manufacture nuances the person never dreamed of conveying. Keep agonizing until you manage to convince yourself that because of all this stress you are going to get cancer and die.

Political. Watch the news on TV. Ignore the national headlines and fasten on a story about a fish-processing plant releasing toxins into the air in a remote, barely inhabited Arctic village. Be certain these toxins are finding their way to your house, and you are going to get cancer and die.

Economic. Buy a stock that drops and leaves you without a nickel to your name (i.e., you can't hack a third week at Club Med). Work long into the night trying to balance your budget. Get a terrible headache and take aspirin. Be positive the pills are eating away at your digestive tract, and you are going to get cancer and die.

What to Do if You Run Out of Worries

Engaging in everyday conversation with a natural-born Jewish person will provide lots of new material. If that isn't feasible, simply make an enormous big deal out of some existing minor problem, such as:

▶ A slow leak in a tire (you might have a blowout on the highway, and it could be snowing so hard a tractor-trailer couldn't stop, and you'd get hit and die).

▶ An ingrown toenail (it could get bad enough so you'd have to wear special shoes. But those wouldn't go with your business clothes, and you'd be fired for having a poor image. Then you'd lose your medical insurance, get blood poisoning, and die).

▶ An overdrawn account (creditors would foreclose, your house would be boarded up, you'd break in to retrieve something you forgot, cut yourself on a rusty nail, get lockjaw, and die).

VACATIONING

▼

When you have vacation time coming up, don't start getting excited about Aspen or Europe. Jews vacation primarily on tropical islands. You are not permitted to enjoy these trips; you will be too busy complaining.

Follow these time-honored rules:

1. Upon landing at your island, be surprised that the local airport isn't air-conditioned.

2. Grumble about the impoverished neighborhoods you pass through on your way to the hotel. Tell the tour guide you didn't come here to be depressed.

3. Run out at dawn to drape towels over the best beach chairs, even if you have no intention of sitting in them. What if you change your mind?

4. Fill your beach bag with every sun protector known to modern science. Smear your body every five minutes. Complain that you're not getting a tan.

5. Be outraged that the natives don't have Sweet 'n Low.

6. Worry about crime, bugs, and your drinking water. Know the scientific terms for all the bacteria the water probably contains, and discuss them with other vacationers. Trade cute names for travelers' diarrhea.

7. Have a minor medical emergency that forces you to get treatment in a ramshackle local hospital. This will be good for years of horror stories.

Summer Vacations

In summer, when the tropics are much too hot for Jews, we occasionally spend a week or weekend at a local resort area. At these times, our activities consist of *eating, sitting, eating* and *shopping,* followed by some more *eating.*

Things Jews don't do at resorts:

▶ Go to un-air-conditioned summer theaters

▶ Play miniature golf

▶ Buy souvenirs with the place-name on them

▶ Swim in lakes

▶ Catch fish and eat them

▶ Get into ballgames with other vacationers

▶ Collect driftwood

SPORTS

▼

T o be appropriate for a Jewish person to engage in, a sport must be noisy, competitive and expensive. Under no circumstance should a sport:

- Involve *earth*.

- Need to be played in *freezing weather* (below 80 degrees).

- Draw *blood*.

- Require a *shared water bottle*.

Favorite Jewish sports include:

- Tennis

- Racquetball

- Ping-Pong

▶ Comparing cars

- Comparing car leases

OTHER LEISURE-TIME ACTIVITIES

▼

Pastimes you always thought were relaxing will now be the opposite. Where you once sat back and let yourself be entertained, you must now contribute.

TV

You will have to discard your pre-Jewish habit of passive viewing or your new family will assume you are depressed or sick. The TV screen is meant to provide discussion material.

Hollywood celebrities are a prime topic. You will be expected to join the fun as everyone:

▶ Argues about who that is on the screen.

▶ Reminisces about her movies or TV series.

▶ Details the plot of every movie or series episode she appeared in.

▶ Wails about how awful she looks.

▶ Swaps stories of who they know who knows her cousin's doorman.

▶ Bickers over who in the family does, used to or will someday resemble her.

TV PROGRAMS JEWS NEVER WATCH

▶ *This Old House*

▶ *America's Most Wanted*

▶ *Wrestlemania*

▶ *The Barbara Mandrell Show*

▶ *Speedway Sunday*

A popular thing to watch is car commercials. You must learn to be really enthusiastic about these. Get up and join your relatives as they move close to the screen to examine the new models. Contribute to the ensuing critique by describing your friends' experiences with their cars. Relate frightening stories about how unsafe the manufacturing process is. Passionately argue about which model everyone is going to buy next.

Reading

Your new Jewish family expects you to be as well-read as they are, so keep up with the new books the same way they do.

Reserve a hot best-seller at the library. Complain about how long it takes to get it. Complain about how little time they give you to read it. Complain about the overdue fine. Hate the book.

Magazines You May Not Subscribe To

▸ *Modern Maturity*

▸ *Jobber Topics*

▸ *Soap Opera Digest*

▸ *Super Service Station*

▸ *Argosy*

WEEKEND FUN

▼

Your new family will always spend Saturday night in the same delightful manner. Here's how to be an effective participant.

1. On Friday, buy a paper. Read the restaurant reviews. Phone the highest-rated one and make a reservation for 8:00 Saturday night.

2. Arrive at 8:10. Indignantly ask why your table isn't ready. Be horrified at the size of the crowd waiting at the bar.

3. At 8:15, start to badger the headwaiter.

4. At 8:30, announce that the place is poorly run.

5. At 8:45, threaten to write a letter to the paper.

6. When you're finally seated, criticize the table, the food and the service.

7. Repeat all steps the following week.

An alternate Saturday night activity is to make several restaurant reservations and select at your leisure. Don't bother canceling the ones you won't keep. You don't want to waste your evening making phone calls.

HAVING PEOPLE OVER

▼

Y ou must shed any pollyanna illusions remaining from your pre-Jewish years about the purpose of entertaining. A Jewish person would never invite people over for ridiculous reasons like *having fun* or *treating friends*.

Appropriate reasons include:

▶ Guilt. (The same person has hosted the last three Thanksgivings, and it wasn't you.)

▶ Pain. (Someone copied your chocolate crème brûlée, and hers came out better.)

▶ Obligation. (Everybody in your body-sculpting class has done a lunch, and you're getting looks.)

▶ Duty. (Your child is the only one in his grade who hasn't had a theme birthday party exciting enough for the newspaper to cover.)

▶ Resentment. (Your cousin had the gall to imply that only she can do lobster right, when you're the one who's brilliant at it.)

▶ Pressure. (Your parents-in-law call daily to see if you've set the date for their surprise anniversary party.)

Your New Host/Hostess Vocabulary

party something non-Jews "have," "throw" or "give," and Jews "make."

lovelynote a written message of thanks that follows a party, weekend, or other absolutely fabulous occasion. Its main use is for the recipient to boast of getting it. ("I had a lovelynote from my daughter-in-law.") Lovelynotes are the only kind Jews ever receive.

Sylvia the home of a couple in which that is the woman's name. ("Are we going to Mildred Saturday?" "No, we're going to Sylvia.")

Sweet 'n Low has replaced *saccharin* as the generic term for artificial sweetener. When a guest asks "Do you have Sweet 'n Low?" the correct answer isn't "No, I have Equal," but "Yes."

THE POLITICS OF ENTERTAINING

▼

Far from being fun, entertaining is a power play. As host, you are President-for-a-Day. This leaves guests in the position of having to please you, flatter you, compete for your attention, and pretend to be closer to you than anyone else there.

So you can't blame them for reacting by engaging in some power games of their own, with you and with one another.

The Counterfeit-Concern Ploy

You're all sitting around the family room. Estelle, a guest, asks several people, one by one, whether they're cold. They all say no. "The air conditioner isn't blowing on you?" she asks. They shake their heads. Estelle nods, relieved that everybody is comfortable, but still looks troubled. She waits patiently.

Finally someone says, "Are *you* cold, Estelle? Maybe we should turn the air conditioner off." "That's a good idea," Estelle says.

The Real-Thing Regatta

Variation A: Everybody is happily snarfing down your wonderful lunch when someone says, "Look—poor Flo spilled soup on her silk blouse."

Flo must now either admit she's wearing polyester or undergo the seltzer-and-angst ritual of removing a spot from silk. If she tries to hedge, someone else will do the follow-up: "Do you think it'll come out, Flo?"

Variation B: You're asked, "Do you have a little Hellman's for this sandwich?"

The speaker wants to contrast her fine taste with your minginess when you bring out your Ann Page mayo. Don't get too excited if you happen to have Hellman's. She'll get you on something else.

The Close Call

A guest slips on a drop of water on the kitchen floor. She catches herself, but her gasp can be heard in Peru. After the Oh-my-God chorus, the Are-you-all-right refrain, and the No-wonder-she-slipped-this-floor's-sopping-wet reprise, the incident is forgotten.

But only for ten minutes.

Each new arrival will be warned about the dangerous floor. He or she will question the victim. Similar experiences will be related, escalating in severity.

When it's time to leave, each guest will remind you to be sure to do something about that death-trap floor.

Outdoor Entertaining

The Cookout, or *bobbycue*, is a casual form of care-free outdoor entertaining, the object of which is to go to far more trouble than if you were serving a meal indoors. These parties take place in boiling-hot weather and usually include young children, who run inside with the mustard, ketchup and melting desserts that you had planned an outdoor dinner to protect your furniture and broadloom from.

Here's how to make a bobbycue:

1. Buy an enormous, heavy, ostentatious, cast-iron gas grill. This device performs the amazing feat of leaving you with plenty of black gunk to clean up, while producing food with no barbecue flavor what-soever. The ideal Jewish outdoor cooking appliance.

2. Make inconvenient trips to distant stores for foods such as custom-ground veal sausage. It would be a crime to serve such delicacies with French's, so be sure to provide four or five varieties of mustard.

3. Serve your paper plates in wicker holders. Plastic cutlery and glasses must be washed and put away to use for the next occasion.

4. Do not spoil anyone's fun by trying to change the subject when your guests debate whether barbecued foods cause cancer.

5. Once the guests have left, keep running out-doors to make sure the grill has cooled, the gas is sealed, and you haven't overlooked any spills that could, Godforbid, attract bugs.

GIFTS

▼

J ews give gifts for every occasion. *Occasions* are not only birthdays and weddings, but also college acceptances, weight loss and the like. Sometimes we ask others' opinions on whether to bring a gift, but we always do, no matter what the advice was.

Some pointers on giving and receiving:

▶ Every gift you get will have strings attached. You will never understand what those are.

▶ Your new relatives would never be so insensitive as to give you a gift certificate. That would deprive you of the joy of criticizing the gift, agonizing over how to say you're exchanging it, schlepping it to the store, and arguing about the store's return policy.

▶ Select gifts for your new family with great care. They won't like anything, but that's no excuse not to drive yourself insane hunting down a better present than anyone else will give.

Gift Guidelines

Type of Gift	Suitable	Unsuitable
Candy	Large, rich chocolate chunks lumpy with nuts, or hand-dipped berries	Gumdrop fruit slices
Flowers	Roses	Arrangement stuck in styrofoam in a cute pottery animal
Wine	Any good French, or a California that was just written up	Cold Duck, Asti Spumante
Food	A nice cheese, exotic fruit, jams with the labels all in Flemish	Petits fours in a decorator tin
Wedding gift	Any useless sterling or crystal item	Breadbox, punch bowl, pop-up toaster
Baby gift	A pink dress or blue suit that has to be dry-cleaned	A battery-operated animal that clacks around the floor and bangs into walls

Part 4

YOUR NEW JEWISH BODY

FEEDING YOUR NEW JEWISH STOMACH

▼

Y ou can't have failed to notice that everyone in your new family is, to say the ridiculous least, body-conscious. Males and females from infancy to passing away are obsessed with the workings of their bodies —and with everything that journeys through them.

Toxic Substances

The modern Jewish digestive system thrives on simple, natural foods. Staples such as tortellini, pesto, rack of lamb, radicchio, smoked trout, raspberry vinaigrette and Sedutto make up the average diet.

There are, however, three life-threatening substances that the Jewish stomach must never ingest.

Non-Diet Soda. You needn't worry when in someone's home. Any regular soda is kept in a separate refrigerator and drunk only by the landscaper. But in a public place, you can't be too careful. A Jewish person wouldn't dream of trusting a restaurant soda to be diet. Upon requesting and being served such a drink, you must follow this procedure:

1. Ask the waiter if he's sure it's diet.
2. Taste it. Taste it again. Frown.

3. Have the person next to you taste it.

4. If there's regular soda at the table, taste that. Let your neighbor compare, too. If there's no non-diet, order some. Remember to make sure you're not billed for it.

Non-Decaf Coffee. Follow the steps above anytime you are served alleged decaffeinated coffee outside of home. Every Jewish family has at least one "expert," and he or she will be glad to sample your cup and render a verdict. Don't trust that opinion either, of course. The expert can't afford the loss of face caused by betraying a doubt. During the whole procedure, keep warning everyone that you're going to be up all night. By the time you've had enough real coffee to satisfy yourself that it's decaf you were served, you certainly will be.

Cream. Jews don't put such a thing in their coffee. You have every right to be irritated if a waitress doesn't know this simple fact. Have her take the cream pitcher away and bring milk. Sniff if. Check for specks. Examine the dispenser with distaste. Decide to drink the coffee black.

Chinese Food

For no reason that has ever been clear to anyone, Jewish people adore Chinese food . . . so if you have anything against it, you'll have to pretend otherwise.

As foreign as caffeine and cream are to our bodies, soy sauce is our cure. Never mind chicken soup; when Jews need comfort, solace or medicinal nourishment, we dive for Moo Shu Pork.

Chinese treats may be enjoyed anytime, but there are two nights on which Jews flock to Chinese restaurants: Thursday (because it's the housekeeper's night off) and Sunday (because we just do).

Two No-Win Negotiations

▶ **1. (Loser: The Waiter)** You are in a Szechuan restaurant. Hot-and-spicy dishes are starred on the menu. Different-color stars indicate grades of spiciness.

Someone in your group asks the waiter how hot a certain dish really is: very, very hot or just hot? Someone else asks whether medium-hot means more medium or more hot.

The waiter does his best to answer these questions. He asks everyone how much spiciness is desired and makes careful notes. Each diner insists on plenty of spice. No one wants food that's too mild. Tales are swapped about the blandness of Szechuan dishes at other restaurants.

When the food comes, everyone sends it back because it's much too hot.

▶ **2. (Loser: You)** You're in someone's kitchen deciding on a takeout order. Foods are suggested. Everyone seems to deliberate before picking.

You're asked what you'd like. You say everything they've chosen sounds great. They press.
There must be *something* you want.

Eager to be polite, you demur. You're told you
might as well pick, since another dish is needed and
everyone else has named something.

Clearly, it would be rude not to contribute.
Beef with snow peas, you say.

There's a thunderclap of silence. Everyone
looks over or around you. Chairs squeak.

Finally someone points out that there's a beef
dish already, two if you count the Land and Sea.

You don't know what to do. Sweating, you suggest peanut chicken.

No. Anita has diverticulitis. No nuts.

Someone else says, Let's get this over with,
how about another large spare ribs? They all turn to
you for agreement.

You'd agree at this point to chopped ashtrays in
garlic sauce. You sigh in relief and nod.

Eventually you will realize that, as with Roz's
parties, this game is ancient. These people were
ordering Chinese food together when you still

hot drink something Jews press on you in cir-
cumstances where non-Jews would provide a *real*
drink (after a car accident or Doberman attack).

coffee a meal, served at any time of the day or
evening, that consists of at least two kinds of
pastry, cookies and sliced fruit. The fruit cancels
out the calories in the pastry.

thought sesame was something on a Big Mac bun.
They always order the same dishes. And they always end up getting another large spare ribs.

Sharing

In your new family, this term applies not only to
Chinese entrées but also to the protocol you must ob-
serve when your meal doesn't agree with you.

Situation

You've eaten out with a relative. Later, you have a
gastrointestinal upset.

Old Behavior. You take Pepto-Bismol or Kaopectate
and go back to sleep.

New Behavior. Immediately call the person you ate
with, no matter what time it is, and describe your
symptoms in detail. The two of you will review and
compare everything you ate, and isolate the likely
cause. It's helpful if you recall that one of these
foods didn't taste right, and that you knew as soon
as you swallowed it that you shouldn't have.

Caring for the Rest of Your New Jewish Body

▼

There's nothing we Jews relish more than medical problems — describing them, second-guessing doctors about them, imagining them, fearing them, having them. You will need to develop this consuming interest yourself. You will also find that the ailments you do have will be different from those of your pre-Jewish years. Never again will you have a simple *cold*. It will be a *chest cold* or *head cold*. In a Jewish family, you can also have a cold in your *back* or *eye*. Don't question these conclusions. All Jews are born diagnosticians.

To prepare for your future colds, you'll have to learn some new behavior.

▶ When someone gets a cold, the whole family has to figure out where it came from. If you're fingered as the carrier because you sneezed once, you must accept the guilt. This is a very damning position for a Jewish person to be in. Don't be surprised to find yourself really nauseous over it.

▶ Always warn people, "Don't kiss me — I have a cold." This is a cardinal rule, even though you and most of the population and the entire AMA believe that a cold is contagious mainly during incubation. You are all wrong.

▶ A family with a new baby knows you'll cancel plans with them ifGodforbid you come down with a cold. This expectation remains in effect until the child votes.

As your body begins its Jewish functioning, you will swap old problems for new ones.

You can no longer get:	But you can get:
Pleurisy	A pinched nerve
A shaving cut	Diabetes
Warts	A hiatus hernia
A black eye	A paper cut
Herpes	Depression
An electric shock	Angina
A cut from a can lid	Gas
A toothache	The *symptoms* of any ailment whatsoever

Your Jewish Emotions

Perhaps you've noticed that most Jewish medical problems are created or aggravated by stress, anger, tension and worry.

We have spent many lifetimes perfecting the emotional minefield that maintains this brain/body axis. It's your responsibility to internalize the time-tested mosaic of Jewish feelings that makes you truly one of us, within and without.

Always:	Never:
Agonize	Be satisfied
Resent	Think anything is fair
Be disappointed	Be a good sport
Gloat	Feel undeserving
Get even	Let go of a grudge
Suffer	Ease up
Be positive something terrible is going to happen	Acknowledge the possibility of any light at the end of a tunnel

How to Choose a Doctor

Any doctor whose name doesn't draw an awestruck gasp when people hear you have an appointment with him is not famous enough to treat you. This may be the reason Jews tend not to have sudden illnesses; so much research is necessary to find an acceptably unavailable physician for a particular problem.

To be qualified to treat you, a doctor must:

▶ Be the most arrogant, condescending sonofabitch you ever met.

▶ Have a narrow specialty, such as thumb surgery or aortic valve replacement.

▶ Be booked solid for the foreseeable future. (If he has openings when you call, hang up immediately.)

▶ Agree to squeeze you in only because someone with pull phoned him for you.

▶ Keep you waiting at least three hours.

▶ Ridicule any other doctor who told you anything.

▶ Seem surprised that you have questions, and rush you out of his office without anwering them.

▶ Send you an outrageous bill.

The Medicine Chest

The most important part of the most important room in a Jewish home, the medicine chest is always fully stocked with impressive prescriptions. But don't count on finding the products you were accustomed to in your pre-Jewish days.

You will find:	But not:
Elavil	Fasteeth
Extra-strength everything	Toothbrushes with rubber gum stimulators
Jolen Creme Bleach	Vicks Vap-O-Rub
Unwaxed dental floss	Razor blades
Maalox	Feen-A-Mint
Rectal Desitin	Aspergum
Every laxative there is	Tums

Your New Outlook on Hospitals and Illness

It's a toss-up whether Jews spend more of their time in restaurants or in hospitals. We're enthusiastic about both, but hospitals have the advantage of providing lots to worry about.

In any case, as a member of a Jewish family, you'll have to spend time in them, too. (Not, Godforbid, as a patient. Of 950 Jews in the average medical center at any moment, 918 are visitors. None, beneath the rank of Attending Physician, are staff.)

ONLY
TWO
GUESTS
PER
PATIENT

Here's what will be expected of you:

▶ Know the visiting hours, medical/surgical/maternity floor designations, and the location of the nearest bakery to all hospitals in your area. (*Area* is defined as your state, and all contiguous states.)

▶ Learn the tricks for getting around the two-visitors-only rule. After you've been in the family awhile, you'll be expected to contribute some new ones.

▶ Be prepared to leave whatever you're doing to accompany your spouse to the hospital when a relative is admitted. If you're trying a case before the Supreme Court and the patient is an eighty-year-old who had a little chest pain after a huge French meal, this still applies.

▶ Never contradict your spouse when he/she tells someone the patient was "rushed to the hospital." This is perfectly accurate even if he walked over in his golf pants.

▶ Never visit without pastry—especially if the patient is on a restricted diet, since there won't be any decent snacks for guests on his meal trays.

▶ Make sure the patient isn't placed with a room-mate whose condition could depress him or his guests.

▶ Remember, it's rude to ignore the roommate and his visitors. Find out their first names im-mediately. Enough pastry should be on hand at all times for both visiting groups. If you arrive and find the roommate without company, it's your duty to cheer him. Draw him out by asking about his condition. Don't be reluctant to mention that you've known people who died of it.

▶ Educate your relative and his roommate on the hideous side effects of their medications. Share any rumors you hear about the hospital's negligence.

Your Hospital Vocabulary

major surgery any surgery undergone by a Jew-ish person.

thenurse a generic term for whatever resource is needed. ("Ask thenurse why there's no des-sert on his tray." Or, "He needs a bigger TV. Tell thenurse.")

agony discomfort. ("They changed Sheila's ban-dage. She was in agony.")

discomfort agony ("Thenurse told Marvin to ex-pect discomfort with the colonoscopy.")

▶ If the patient is in Intensive Care, don't worry about those ridiculous ICU visiting regulations. Of course "immediate family" includes his club.

Medical Prestige

You must strive to adopt a whole new view of illness and its treatment. You used to feel sympathy and concern for a sick person; now you will need to be impressed. The more complicated the sickness, the more admiring you must be. With years of experience, you should even be able to manage genuine envy.

A patient gains extra prestige when:

▶ The ailment takes its most extreme form. (Perhaps even more extreme than was previously possible. Only Jews can have triple pneumonia or a septuple bypass.)

▶ The problem can't be diagnosed. "The Doctors don't know what's wrong with her" is as awe-inspiring a statement as can be made at a bridge game. (*The Doctors*, incidentally, are a single entity, a body of learned men who move about and adjudicate as a unit, like bundled cigars.)

▶ He's waiting for the results of what is always a "battery of tests." You can grab some prestige yourself by becoming a waiter or sub-waiter (the person who's waiting to hear from the person who's waiting to hear from the patient, who's waiting to hear from The Doctors).

▶ His doctor has status. It's not enough just to be a specialist; Jews don't go to doctors who aren't specialists. The status doctor must be the "top man in the field." Often he's also one of the "top five in the country." As of now, there are 348 top five urologists in the country.

▶ Certain foods are prohibited. The restriction must be unique enough so the patient can, for example, announce in a restaurant, "Take away that lasagna. The oregano could kill me." For maximum effect, the statement should be made by someone else: "Keep those scallops away from Rose. She could convulse."

When Someone Is Sick in the Hospital

Don't Say:	Say:
"I'm so sorry."	"I'm not surprised."
"I hope you feel better."	"What are they giving you?"
"That should help."	"That's the worst thing they could do."
"Can I do anything for you?"	"Oh, my God. I was with you last week."

SHE'S SICK? OH NO! I KISSED HER!

DEATH

▼

Jews do not *die*. We *pass away* or are *gone* or *lost*. The word *anything* is used to signify the possibility of death ("IfGodforbid anything should happen to Hy . . .").

Part 5

BUILDING YOUR
NEW JEWISH
ECONOMIC
PERSPECTIVE

MONEY

▼

Undoubtedly you are intimidated by this issue, given all the clichés about Jews' obsession with money. Relax—this is a fallacy. We're not obsessed with it. We've long since accepted its place in our lives; we simply make ourselves nauseous about everything else *while* dealing with money.

The true priorities of Jewish life are:

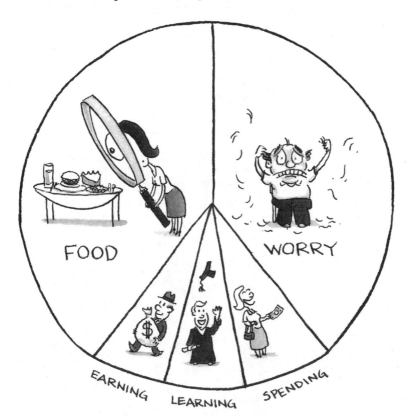

THE JOB

▼

Jews do not *work*. We *have a business* or are *in business* or are *with* a company. Rather than being *employed by* that company, we *have a position* there.

To be right for a Jewish person, a job must:

▶ Be stressful.

▶ Necessitate numerous argumentative meetings.

▶ Have ironclad deadlines that are never met.

▶ Involve tiers of people who contradict one another's instructions.

▶ Teeter on an intricate pyramid of favors owed and expected.

▶ Include groups of subordinates crowded together who are always at each other's throats.

▶ Involve problems that not only can't be defined but create worse problems as you try to define them.

▶ Have worst-case scenarios that always come true.

Things You Can Count on Hearing

These employment- and money-related phrases will fall around you with the steady constancy of rain:

▶ "It's who you know." (Intoned with a sage nod every time someone in the family gets, or fails to get, a hot job.)
▶ "You'll have it to fall back on." (Said while pushing every student in the family toward a teaching degree, whether the kid is interested in ballet, architecture or whaling.)
▶ "You get what you pay for." (Said accusingly to the person responsible for buying an item, whatever the cost, that has just worn out or broken.)
▶ "How can you go wrong?" (Demanded in astonishment when you've just declined to buy three cases of kiwi fruit at an irresistible discount.)
▶ "It's an investment." (Used to explain spending $295 on a blouse. It is anti-Semitic to ask, "In what?")

OCCUPATIONAL LOGISTICS AND STRATEGY

▼

People Skills

In your new work life as a Jewish person, you will have to banish such absurd concepts as *tact, diplomacy* and *fair play*. These are sweet, but they don't accomplish anything.

Our Jewish repertoire of people skills has served us well for centuries. It will serve you, too, however you earn your living.

These four methodologies constitute all you'll ever need to know about dealing with people in your work, be they associates, clients, subordinates, patients, pupils, suppliers or customers. The techniques may be used singly, or they may be alternated or combined. Of course, they all address the same objective, the only one that matters to you now that you're Jewish: *getting your way.*

Infuriate them. Condescend. Belittle. Have preposterous expectations. Remember their goofs. Notice their odd habits. Hate their taste. Question their sincerity. Claim not to understand what they want from you. Wonder aloud why they're wasting your time. Pretend they're not making sense.

Love them to bitty-bits. Grin. Hug. Flatter. Ask sensitive, probing, personal questions. Understand their pain. Pat their hand. Fluff their hair. Call them by adorable, original pet names. Have private jokes. Remember everything they say. Give surprises. Make confessions. Love their favorites. Send them fruit/cartoons/samples/tickets/wine.

Pile on guilt. Plead. Be sorry, sheepish. Cock your head. Sniff. Squeeze their shoulder. Apologize with eloquence, humor, desperation. Hint at your poverty. Share your problems. Need their assistance. Praise their talent. Beg for their understanding. Envy their luck. Exaggerate your contribution.

Drive them berserk. Call them by the wrong name, a different one each time. Forget a third of what they tell you. Confuse their achievements with someone else's. Ask questions and ignore the answers. Call them repeatedly, then be unavailable when they call back. Change a date. Change your mind. Change their instructions/appointment/assignment/order.

Business Travel

1. So you won't have to waste time waiting for luggage when your plane lands, bring several carry-on bags. Make sure they're cumbersome, awkward, heavy, and take up a lot of room. Hold up the line in the jetway as you rearrange them.

Stow them so that any space your seatmates might need is taken.

2. On the plane, make plenty of calls on the cellular phone. (Work into each conversation where you're calling from.) When the phone begins to hiss and fade, let your seatmates have their turn.

3. At the hotel, demand every convenience you rely on at home. Insist on getting your breakfast before your 6:00 A.M. jog, whether Room Service is open or not. There's no reason you shouldn't take advantage of people just because you're in a different town.

4. Expect perfect service on messages and phone calls. Be outraged when no one comes into the sauna to find you.

Professional Courtesy

If you're a professional, your new friends and relatives know you will be honored to make your service available to them at little or no charge. Here's how to handle people who won't be paying your usual fee:

▶ Make sure they have trouble getting an appointment. Feel free to change or cancel it. When they come, warn them you're pressed for time. Be distracted.

▶ Send them an itemized bill, even if they won't be paying anything. Next to each service, write "No charge."

▶ When you can get away with it, bill for part of the fee. Make a big deal on the bill about the discount. Really smack them between the eyes with what they would have paid without it.

▶ Keep saying how lucky they are to have you.

▶ Be apoplectic anytime a professional has the gall to send *you* a bill.

Some Additions to Your Economic Vocabulary

biznizz a woman's workplace. ("Does your mother still go to biznizz?")

pockabook what a woman carries for social occasions or biznizz.

know from be an expert in. ("Helen is an assistant buyer. She knows from suits.")

not know from be totally ignorant of. ("Helen is a suit buyer. She doesn't know from blouses.")

senior-citizen discount a price reduction for a non-Jewish old person.

rock the absolutely lowest possible price a seller will accept.

steal below *rock*.

WHAT A STEAL! I DIDN'T EVEN PAY ROCK!

NETWORKING

▼

As you begin to think like a Jewish person, you'll discover how divine it feels to be owed a favor. Networking is a fine way to build a collection of favors receivable.

SITUATION

A friend is looking for a job. You happen to overhear someone mention an opening.

Old Behavior: You pass along the lead.

New Behavior: Tell your friend you have confidential information about a once-in-a-lifetime opportunity. Make sure he understands how much trouble it was to find this out. Keep asking if he got an interview, if he had the interview, if he's heard anything yet. If he doesn't get the job, imply that he didn't pursue it correctly. If he gets it, take full credit.

AMALGAMATED ANAGRAM HAS AN OPENING.

I TALKED TO MY CONTACTS...
...PULLED SOME STRINGS...
...GOT AN INSIDE TIP...
CALL AMALGAMATED ANAGRAM.

CONSUMERISM

▼

Every Jewish family has one or more Professional Consumers. These mavens know all the best stores and services. When you buy something, they know where you could have gotten it cheaper, why it was a poor choice anyhow, and what you should have picked instead for less money.

It's easy to make errors that help PCs behave even more obnoxiously than they routinely do. Step carefully, lest you be ambushed.

Do Not:

▶ Mention in a PC's presence which bakery, butcher, hairdresser, mechanic or piano tuner you patronize. He'll be completely familiar with its limitations and will explain in detail why it isn't nearly as good as the one he uses.

▶ Change to his. In three months he'll be asking why you're dumb enough to keep patronizing such a terrible place.

YOU WON'T SEE A JEWISH PERSON SPEND DOLLAR ONE AT:

▸ Channel Home Centers
▸ A pancake supper
▸ The Poconos
▸ A jumble sale
▸ J.C. Penney's
▸ Academy Auto Parts
▸ Dunkin' Donuts
▸ A dude ranch
▸ A 7-Eleven
▸ H & R Block

▶ Try to top him. You can't. Your goal is simply to find a good bakery or mechanic. The PC's goal is to be able to say he has a better one.

▶ Get trapped into recommending a place if a PC asks you to. Not only won't he like it, but he'll go on often — at length, and in front of as many people as possible — about how bad it was and how much trouble this fiasco caused him. He'll expect you to sympathize.

Part 6

RAISING YOUR JEWISH CHILD

NAMING YOUR CHILDREN

▼

I n your new Jewish family, name negotiations will begin long before the first baby arrives or is even conceived. Consider yourself fortunate if your in-laws aren't hissing "Sophie!" and "Herschel!" into your ear as you walk down the aisle.

First names fall into two categories:

Guilt — Harold, Rose, Esther
Nouvelle — Nicholas, Michelle, Justin

This is also true of your new Jewish surname (which you will be known by whether you officially take it or not, regardless of your gender, because Jewish names are always dominant):

Ethnic — Garbstein, Markowitz
Mayonnaised — Kane, Steen, Marks

Thus the permutations for your child's full name range from **nouvelle-nouvelle-mayonnaised**:

Alison Melissa Crane

to **guilt-guilt-ethnic**:

Samuel Seymour Wasserfarb

with the most common choices being mixtures:

Nouvelle-guilt-mayonnaised—Brittany
   Sylvia Rapp
Guilt-nouvelle-ethnic—Nathan Derek
   Glicktenstein
Nouvelle-nouvelle-ethnic—Whitney Jillian
   Frolenkramp

or, where the family is large and the relatives vocal, longer combinations that may include an honorific surname from a past generation:

Nouvelle-guilt-ethnic-mayonnaised — Kristin
   Harriet Hasselowitz Stone
Nouvelle-nouvelle-ethnic-ethnic — Clint Jordan
   Kruchkow Fishkin
Guilt-nouvelle-nouvelle-ethnic — Florence
   Brandi Danielle Polinsky
Guilt-nouvelle-guilt-mayonnaised—Irwin Sean
   Marvin Rice

Finally, there are the combinations produced by hyphenating the parents' surnames, Jewish and Not:

Nouvelle-nouvelle-Jewish-Not—Ryan Kirk
   Smolenoff-Marlow
Nouvelle-guilt-Not-Jewish—Brooke Mildred
   Church-Finkfelder

THE PSYCHOLOGY OF CHILD-RAISING*

▼

Perhaps *you* were raised with discipline and rules . . . where a tantrum might be ignored to teach you a lesson. Never even contemplate such criminal neglect of your Jewish child. You have to hang over your little one like a giant bat. This vigilance must carry into the child's later development, leaving no aspect of his high school and college life unscrutinized, un-listened to, un-harped on, un-nagged about.

Your child will be so grateful to realize, upon becoming a parent, who provided the emotional seedlings that flower then, all ready to nurture the next generation.

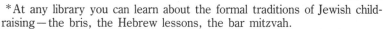

---

*At any library you can learn about the formal traditions of Jewish child-raising — the bris, the Hebrew lessons, the bar mitzvah.

(The circumcision and the adulthood ceremony are actually the same event for the male child, separated by thirteen years. The only differences in the bar mitzvah are these:

▶The rabbi stays longer.

▶There is more food.

▶No cutting is done, aside from the guests' comments about one another's outfits.)

Here we deal not with information readily available elsewhere, but with the crucial real facts that have never until now been codified — the truths without which you might tragically stumble and raise a youngster who is quiet, reasonable and unselfish.

Mixed Messages

You must make certain your child receives the traditional series of these throughout the growth years. How else can he or she achieve the correct *adult* psychological state, i.e., being constantly in therapy and never getting any better?

▶ You're the best/You'll never be good enough.

▶ Eat/Be thin.

▶ We'll take care of you/Grow up.

▶ You can't fail/You can't win.

▶ Save/Spend/Earn/Give/Buy/Keep.

▶ Don't worry/Worry.

Rhetorical Questions

Continually repeated, these become a lifelong lullaby for the Jewish child. They establish and maintain the precarious security that is the Jewish person's birthright. Some favorites you must not omit:

▶ "Do you want to break your neck?"

▶ "This is how you thank us?"

▶ "Are you crazy?"

▶ "You're wearing that?"

▶ "For this I'm spending twenty thousand a year?"

▶ "Who am I, Rockefeller?"

▶ "Are you trying to give me a heart attack?"

EDUCATION

▼

N o school is ever going to come remotely close to approaching any semblance of being the slightest bit good enough for your child. As long as you simply accept this fact from the start, the youngster's education will flow smoothly.

This does not, of course, release you from your obligation to monitor the entire process, from toddler years through adulthood.

You must not fail to:

1. Insist constantly and loudly that the child is bored for lack of challenge.

college a place where children are sent after high school to get impressive decals for the family cars.

2. Rail against the arbitrary unfairness of standardized tests (if your child scores low) or against the ignorance of parents who consider them unfair (if your child aces them).

3. Demand private-school quality from public school, college-level teaching from private school, graduate facilities from college, and the patently impossible from any one-to-one instruction.

Child-Raising Terms You Need to Know

themiddleofthenight a dangerous, otherworldly dimension that can only be escaped by sleeping: "What are you doing up? It's themiddleof-thenight." This question, repeated often and ominously, puts the finishing touch on any neuroses not already established.

ruin your appetite what a food will do if it's spontaneously snacked on, not served by the parent: "Don't eat that sandwich. You'll ruin your appetite."

grateful what your child must be continually re-minded he isn't: "Who else would make you nice onions with your liver? You should be grateful."

knock wood an extra tragedy-banishing mantra added to the usual phraseology when dealing with potentially catastrophic situations involving your child: "Ifgodforbid you don't get into MIT, knock wood . . ."

YOUR CHILD'S FUTURE

▼

I t is your parental responsibility to guide your child to a career that is, or sounds, important. Do not shrink from your vital role in this process. Your Jewish child expects to be nagged, pressured, browbeaten and bludgeoned into a career path. Be creative in applying tactics such as threats, extortion, blackmail and tyranny. Withhold love, money, esteem, approval or whatever will work; you know your child best. Never back down in this crusade. Do you want your child to think you don't care?

Important-Career Areas

▶ Law
▶ Medicine

Acceptable

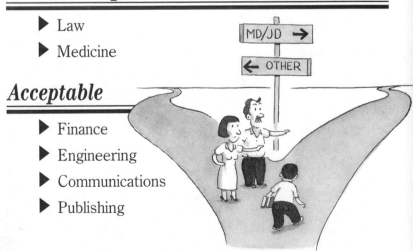

▶ Finance
▶ Engineering
▶ Communications
▶ Publishing

If All Else Fails

- Teaching
- Retailing
- ▶ Social work
- ▶ Manufacturing
- Real estate

Fields You Can Forget About Your Child Ever Entering

- The military
- Automotive
- Chiropractic
- ▶ Midwifery
- Podiatry
- Para-anything

WHEN YOUR CHILD IS
READY TO MARRY

▼

No one in your Jewish family expects you to hide the fact that you hate your child's intended. Indeed, eyebrows would rise if you didn't.

Your relatives will rally around and share your disappointment. They will graciously join you in trashing the person. They will nod knowingly when, in the intended's presence, you ostentatiously button your lip and look skyward.

You can count on this unquestioning support for the best of reasons: they all know that one day, despite their best efforts, they will be in your position. They will strive as desperately as you are striving to transfer their heartbreak over the loss of their child to the handiest target.

It will be your duty to help each of them as they are helping you.

MEETING THE PROSPECTIVE IN-LAWS

▼

This is your last chance to get their child out of your life, so use it well. If that fails, you still have much to gain from this meeting: it's never too soon to begin tipping the familial power balance. Start now, and you'll enjoy years of tactical rewards as the in-laws struggle for equality. With good early work on your part, they might not get to see the first grandchild for months.

1. Invite them onto your turf before they can summon you to theirs.

2. Present the engaged couple with tickets to some event distant enough so they won't barge in on you.

3. Find a way to put the prospective in-laws on the defensive immediately. Telling them to come an hour too late is a favorite. Their first look at the two of you beside your incinerated roast, bravely covering your pain, will pay off for decades.

3. Cross your fingers under the table and murmur something about your child, like "We'll have to plan the wedding around Randall's trial. It's so unfair — you'd think he'd killed someone, instead of just exposing himself." Don't worry about this getting back. Your child knows you would never say such a thing.

4. Don't dwell on the ethics of your behavior for one tiny second. It's for a good cause. And your in-laws would have done it if they'd thought of it first.

THE WEDDING

▼

Surely, you may be thinking, this is one area where you don't need lessons — after all, you experienced your own wedding to a Jewish person, and your child's marriage might not be mixed.

The difference is that you did not experience the wedding from the Jewish dugout.

There is much to be learned that has nothing to do with who your child marries, Jewish or Not . . . but everything to do with *you*, the child's Jewish parents, and how this event bespeaks *your* sophistication, charm and taste.

Who do you think your child's wedding is *for*?

The Negotiations

As in any ethnic group, the bride's family, who are paying for the wedding, decide on the location, catering, and guest list.

In a Jewish family, *decide* is defined as *make an opening offer*.

It is simply not conceivable to a Jewish couple that they can't control their own child's wedding. You must hold this view if your child is the groom, and prepare for it if your child is the bride. Thus the best compromise one can expect between tradition and reality is that the groom's family, whether you or they, will interfere with, second-guess, badger and outshout the bride's on every aspect of the event — in other words, negotiate.

People think a Jewish wedding is planned far in advance of the date because facilities are in demand. This is a myth. It is because months and sometimes years are needed for the rounds of necessary talks.

Topics to be negotiated include (but are not limited to) the following:

▶ Total number of guests

▶ Number of guests from each side

▶ Designation of cardiologist to treat coronaries resulting from battles over this issue

▶ Selection of calligrapher for addressing invitations

▶ Number of unnecessary enclosures in invitations

▶ Tent rental company (see below)

▶ Designation of family member to deal in the time-honored manner with guests who gauchely bring gift to wedding (designee must frown, reluctantly take gift, then look helplessly around for a place to put it)

▶ Photographer

▶ Ostentatiousness of photo album

▶ Number of pictures inanely posed in keyholes

▶ Band

▶ Proportion of contemporary and traditional music

▶ Degree of aggressiveness permitted in urging guests onto the floor for line dances

▶ Hors d'oeuvre buffet

▶ Method of settling arguments among less sophisticated guests about whether this is dinner

▶ Number of entrée choices to be offered

▶ Number of substitute entrées for guests who reject all the choices

▶ Size of tables

▶ Seating assignments

▶ Method of placating guests who hate where you put them

▶ Selection of seat of honor for host family's cleaning lady

▶ Designation of relative to keep loudly announcing that she's one of the family

▶ Florist

▶ Lavishness of flowers

▶ Method of garnering most civic attention for donating flowers to hospital after wedding

The Tent

A tent must be rented for your child's wedding reception, regardless of the indoor facilities available. This ensures that you will spend at least as much money without being deprived of the pleasure of worrying about the weather.

The Bar

A well-stocked bar must include soda, caffeine-free soda, diet soda, club soda, Crème de Cacao, Cherry Heering and Harvey's Bristol Cream. Anything else is optional.

The Viennese Table

You can have a Jewish wedding without a *chuppa* but not without a Viennese Table. And you must be sure to *call* it a Viennese Table. Then it won't matter what other food is served, or how little of it, because all the guests' conversations afterward will go:

> "How was the wedding?"
> "Wonderful. They had a Viennese Table."

The Show-'Em-How-It-Should've-Been Party (For Groom's Parents Only)

Have the party a polite interval after the wedding — say, a week and a half. Invite everyone on your side who came to the wedding, plus everyone who didn't, plus your dry cleaner, hair colorist, and decorator. Invite your son's old girlfriends, so they can see what they missed. Serve Himalayas of spectacular food. Hire a hot band. Hint that another band was lined up, but Mick had a sore throat.

Everyone will leave believing this is how the wedding would have been in the first place, but you were too polite to impose your tastes on your son's new in-laws. And are certainly too polite to admit that this is the reason for *this* party.

Part 7

JOINING IN THE CUSTOMS OF YOUR NEW JEWISH FAMILY

THE BUYING OF THE SUIT

▼

When a man needs a suit, he and his wife go to the store. The salesman and the wife make selections from the rack. The husband tries them on. The wife and salesman discuss the fit, remarking on the fullness, thinness or any asymmetry of the husband's body. The jacket and pants are pulled, tucked, pleated and bunched in assessing the need for tailoring.

Once a suit is chosen, the wife and the store's tailor repeat the fitting procedure and then negotiate a date when the suit will be ready.

On leaving the store, the husband may talk if he wishes.

THE RETURNING OF THE SUIT

T he return visit begins with the berating of the tailor. He claims he could do no better on such shoddy fabric. The salesman is called for. He blames the tailor.

Eventually the salesman, tailor and wife will strike a compromise in which the suit is refitted at no charge and an additional item, such as an unstylish tie or belt, is thrown in. This signals the completion of the ritual.

THE SWIMMER'S MIRACLE

▼

Jews never enter a pool, ocean or lake without following this checklist:

▶ All-over sun block

▶ White goop covering lips and nose

▶ A shirt

▶ A hat

For water that is freezing cold (i.e., below body temperature), we perform this magic trick:

Wading in to the ankles, we bend and scoop water into our hands. We rub it on our shoulders, arms and legs, in that order. This causes our skin to become instantly accustomed to water of any temperature.

THE COLLECTIONS

▼

Jars. This accumulation can take up a whole kitchen cabinet. It serves no purpose, since there is a whateverware container for every type of food. But no Jewish person is capable of throwing out a perfectly good jar.

Shopping Bags. Every Jewish household has in a closet a large shopping bag that contains many more shopping bags. These are acquired from stores and through the Shopping Bag Exchange Program (Paula sends extra Danish home with Belle in a Bloomingdale's bag; Miriam brings Paula more Danish in a Macy's bag).

Wrapping Paper. Gifts are opened carefully, using a pencil to lift the tape, so the paper can be saved. It isn't reused; that would be cheap. But it's a crime to throw away such lovely paper.

EATING OUT

▼

F or Jews, the restaurant experience is a microcosm for life, encompassing all things closest to our hearts—food, money, conversation, competition, manipulation, even worry (will they honor our reservation? Will the soup be hot? Will they have the grapefruit mousse? Will it be as good as last time?).

Restaurant dining has its own set of traditions. These are most unique. In no other aspect of Jewish life will you find conventions so different from yours.

SITUATION 1

You're at a restaurant for dinner. The headwaiter leads your party to a table.

Old Behavior. You sit down, order, enjoy your meal and leave.

New Behavior. Since the first table offered is always inferior, your group must select the one you prefer and tell the headwaiter. If the original table is really poor (near the kitchen or, Godforbid, the air conditioner), you'll need time to recover from the trauma. Sit down, use the ashtrays and napkins, and have a nice drink of water before you move.

SITUATION 2

You're now settled at a table. Adjoining it — within thirty feet, say — is another party having dinner.

Old Behavior. You disregard them.

New Behavior. You must drop the misconception that other diners are uninterested in talking with you. They'd love to hear about restaurants you've been to that are better than this. To be really sociable, ask what they're eating, peer at it, comment on how it looks, and find out why they're leaving anything that's been pushed aside.

SITUATION 3

You're lunching with someone in your new family. He/she orders the stuffed avocado. That sounds good to you.

Old Behavior. You say, "I'll have the same."

New Behavior. Have the chef's salad. Ordering the same dish as your companion is an affront. It implies that he/she isn't welcome to sample your meal, and that you don't wish to show your affection by doing the same.

SITUATION 4

You've ordered a different dish but can't quite bring yourself to eat from your companion's plate. He/she smiles warmly and hands you a forkful.

Old Behavior. You remove the food with your teeth, or transfer it to your own fork.

New Behavior. Take the fork. Smile back. Enclosing the fork in your lips, take the food. Return the fork. Women can leave behind some lipstick for an added touch of warmth. Reciprocate with your fork. Take it back.

Even assimilated non-Jews often forget the crucial last step, which is to be sure your partner sees you using your fork as intimately as he/she just did. Resist the temptation to wipe it off. Short of naming your baby after a living relative, there's no deeper insult to a Jewish person.

What to Bring to the Restaurant

Never leave home without these essentials:

1. A little sweater (in case the air conditioner is on)
2. A matchbook (to put under the table leg if the table isn't steady)
3. A review of the place (so you can start to be disappointed even before you get home)

SITUATION 5

You've taken an elderly relative to dinner. She can't decide what to have.

Old Behavior. You make some suggestions.

New Behavior. Read her the entire menu. Don't leave out any of the helpful descriptions ("served with piping-hot fresh-baked rolls and a garden-crisp salad"). Read it nice and loud. Other patrons may need help deciding, too.

SITUATION 6

Your group is deciding what to order. Each entrée comes with side dishes and salad.

Old Behavior. Everyone selects an entrée, picks a salad dressing, and enjoys whatever vegetables are served.

New Behavior. Your group must ask the waitress what vegetable and potato come with each entrée. Feel free to mix and match to get what you prefer. Have the waitress recite the salad dressings several times. Request one she didn't name. Find out what's in the salad, and make sure she writes down what each person wants left out. If you feel like having something like sliced tomatoes and onions instead, say so. Find out what sauce is served with each entrée. Order that, and any ingredients in the dish that you might not like, on the side. If the waitress is ungracious about any of your instructions, complain that they should learn how to run a restaurant.

Part 8
READINESS TEST

THE TEST

▼

Take this quiz to see if you've learned enough to function in your new Jewish family.

1. There are no Jews living in
   a. sin
   b. El Paso
   c. trailer parks

2. The cleaning lady in a Jewish household is expected to
   a. do windows
   b. make latkes
   c. attend all bar mitzvahs and weddings

3. To make a good pet for a Jewish child, an animal must be
   a. gentle
   b. housebroken
   c. stuffed

4. Jews spend their vacations
   a. sightseeing
   b. sunbathing
   c. discussing where they spent their last vacation and where they'll spend the next

5. A Jewish mouth never
   a. lies
   b. closes
   c. contains gold teeth

6. If there's a hairdresser in your immediate family, you are
    a. up on the newest styles
    b. entitled to free haircuts
    c. not Jewish

7. Wilderness means
    a. no running water
    b. no electricity
    c. no hot-and-sour soup

8. The most popular outdoor sport among Jews is
    a. jogging
    b. tennis
    c. howling over the neighbors' lawn ornaments

9. Jews never drive
    a. unsafely
    b. on Saturdays
    c. eighteen-wheelers

10. A truly unsuitable gift for a Jewish person is
    a. Easter lilies
    b. a crucifix
    c. a Zippo lighter

11. A Jewish skydiver is
    a. careful
    b. insured
    c. an apparition

12. Jews never eat at restaurants that
    a. aren't kosher
    b. cost too much
    c. have paintings for sale

13. No Jewish person in history has ever been known to
    a. become a prostitute
    b. deface a synagogue
    c. remove the back of a TV set

14. There is no such thing as a Jewish
  a. black belt
  b. obscene caller
  c. toll collector

15. Jews never sing
  a. off-key
  b. "Nel Blu di Pinto di Blu"
  c. around a piano bar

16. You won't catch a Jewish person on a
  a. horse
  b. backhoe
  c. toot

17. Jews are ambivalent about
  a. vegetarianism
  b. Jesse Jackson
  c. absolutely nothing

SCORING: Take 1 point for each *a* answer, 2 for each *b*, 3 for each *c*.

39 to 51: Mazel tov! You know a lot about Jews. Either you've studied your loved one's family carefully, out of your desire for true closeness plus your respect for their traditions, or you're from Florida. They'll adore you.

29 to 38: You're not quite there yet, but don't panic. Just remember to do everything louder, longer, and with a lot more butter than you used to.

17 to 28: Sorry. Better go back to page 1 and start again. Or consider getting a divorce and buying a Denny's franchise.

About the Author

M olly Katz, author of seven humorous romance novels, is a former stand-up comedienne who now performs at her word processor. The hours are better for her complexion, and she doesn't need to wear as much jewelry.